Pick-up the Pieces of your Brokenness and Live

Pick-up the Pieces of your Brokenness and Live

Inspirational Messages

Ellie Patrick

To order additional copies of this book, contact:
Xlibris Corporation
1-888-795-4274
www.Xlibris.com
Orders@Xlibris.com
59896

ACKNOWLEDGMENTS

I'm amazed at the goodness of God in that He would pick me to give these words of inspiration to His people. God allowed Mrs. Sue Synder entrance into my life to assist me with love and grace in the same way Timothy, Philemon, and others assisted Paul in his mission to build the Body of Christ. Thanks so much HGG.

I give double honor to my leaders Bishop Harold and Prophetess Brenda Ray for teaching me the heart of God. Their prayers and love is more than I can express. God blessed me more when He gave them to me. I love and respect you both. Blessing to   my brothers and sisters at Redemptive Life Fellowship.

I give special thanks to the following persons: My mom and dad, Rev. Freddie and Mary Thornton, Andrena St.Joe-Louis, Katherine Berry, Sabrina and Loretta Thornton, all are my favorite sisters. (Well, one of you know the real deal). Michael and Erica, my babies (I know you both are grown) thanks for loving me like you do. Thanks for understanding that I wasn't perfect yet prefered to be your Mom. The both of you are blessed and remarkably favored by God.

Thanks, Myra Dixon, Romanda Cobia, Owena Brown, Elder Stella Butts (You kept me alive), Mr. & Mrs. Earl and Ester Willis, of San Diego, California, Andrea Perkins, and Delia Powell, your unique way of ministering to me is always on time. Last but not at all the least, the man God has given me to take me on to the finish line, Mr. Paul Holliday. You are the kind of blessing that must be discerned or one can easily overlook a tremendous gift God has given to the world.

Blessings and Peace to all my readers and supporters.

I yet rise to meet Him.

FOREWORD

All through the holy bible we read stories of biblical characters that illustrate to us that pain is not our permanent address.

Through these pages you will gain great insight on how you too can pick up the pieces of your brokenness and Live A Victorious Life.

Ellie's story lets us know that after every death experience there is resurrection. Live!

Dr. Brenda Ray
Co-Pastor
Redemptive Life Fellowship,
West Palm Beach, Florida

FOREWORD

"ELLIE"

If I had one gift to give to all my family and friends it would be Ellie. Ellie is the best example of someone who reveals the heart of God. Her spirit is so sensitive to Him. She has taught me how to love the Lord in a way that is so child-like and personal. I now have a faith that can believe for anything. Talking to her is like talking to God's closest and best friend. She knows Him so very well. Ellie's messages are from the heart of God and her desire is to tell God's people how deep, wide and high His love is for them. She is a chosen vessel that has been refined in the fire. She is so pure and humble. I consider her the most precious gift that God has given to reveal Himself to me.

Sue Snyder
Free Chapel Worship Center, Gainesville Georgia
Pastor, Jentezen Franklin

FOREWORD

In a world filled with fear, hopelessness and opression; the true saints of God are finding faith to believe for God's promises. They are receiving a grace to walk a lifestyle of strength, encouragement and comfort as Holy Spirit makes the Word of God come alive in their hearts. He's imparting a joy that's "unspeakable and full of glory". God is raising up a Jacob generation who will seek God until He can be found. There is a prophetic generation who will build the body of Christ in the last days.

It is my privilege to witness these truths in a woman who hears from God and allows the River of God to flow out of her innermost being to all who will read and listen. Thanks Ellie, for giving these words of hope to the body of Christ in this hour. I pray Christ's heart is experienced by all who read these unique and timely messages from the Father.

Pastor David Reynolds

When my husband passed away, I was so afraid of my future outcome. I asked God, "What am I going to do with myself? I feel like I can't go on without him." God said, "Don't ever be afraid of living because you will never have a life." Pick up the pieces of your brokenness and *live*!

There are days when I just want Him to hold me so tight until all my fears go away. There are times when I want to hear Him say exclusively to me, "Out of all the others, you are Mine! You are My favorite!" Sometimes I just want to crawl up in His lap and throw my arms around His shoulders and say, "Daddy, oh Daddy, it's you whom I love more than anyone or anything. I just do, Lord. I really do." Then there are days I abandon my phone, TV, and friends so He can have *all* my attention. I say to Him, "I don't know what I would do without you. If you were to leave me, I'd go crazy." I don't know how much He means to you, but He's all I got. He's all I need. He's all I've *ever* wanted.

While riding the bus to work, I wondered how many people really know who is sitting next to them. If they did, would they ask for an autograph? Would they share their hopes and dreams? Would they be kinder? Would they be more respectful? Introduce yourself to the world. Get to know those among you so when you make it, they'll have to pause and say, "I knew it! I knew it!"

Regardless of how undesirable or undeserving you might feel, God still wants you.

Have you ever wondered what the woman with the *issue* of blood said to Jesus on the day her faith made her whole? The Bible says she told Him all the truth. Did she tell Him how lonely she'd been? How unwanted and unloved she felt? How long it took between visits for her family to return? Did she tell Him how many nights and days she cried? Nonetheless, Jesus patiently listened to approximately twelve years of her personal struggles. He *heard* her *issues*. He will *hear* yours. The next time you talk to Him, tell Him *all* the truth. Tell Him everything.

Do whatever it takes to please the Lord even if it means letting go of some things you hold dear to your heart. Like Abraham, He may ask you for your Isaac. This is the reason He wants to perfect us and know what's in our hearts. Surrender to Him anything He wants because it will be *greater* later.

Like the sands on the beach, so are God's thoughts concerning you.

All is forgotten and forgiven. He doesn't remember anything. As far as the east is from the west, so far are your sins removed. Now, forgive yourself and move on.

Before your momma ever met your daddy, God knew you. He called you and gave you an assignment. Don't let Him down; He's invested too much into your future.

One day God asked Jeremiah what he saw, and Jeremiah told God what he had seen. God said, "You have seen right. And because of your accurate perception, I am ready to perform My word." Whenever we answer him through our eyes of faith, our answer is always right. So the next time He asks you, "How's the marriage, the children, the job, the relationship between the both of you?" Say, "It's good." Then watch Him get to work on your behalf.

May the peace of God cover you like a blanket. May His love for you be felt throughout your day. May His grace carry you into places you never thought you would go. May He remind you in some way today that His mercy for you is new every morning. May He show you today that there is absolutely nothing He can't do.

If there is a longing in your heart for an empty place to be filled, know that another person, another toy, or another outfit can't occupy your empty space. Only He can fill the void and make you whole again. So the next time your heart longs for something, say to Him, "Come to my place and fill this empty space."

He sees all the effort you put into the assignment He's given you. He sees how so many times you just wanted to throw in the towel. He also knows how many times you just kept going in spite of the pain. *So* He told me to tell you, "*Great job*" and that "your *labor* is *not* in *vain*."

When was the last time you had a serious heart checkup? Not at the doctor's office but one with you and Him. I did a few days ago, and I discovered something in me that made me weep before Him. I asked Him to please fix my heart and to not leave me this way. While He worked on my heart, I asked Him to wash me. Wash here. Wash there. Don't forget here. Especially there, Lord. Try it today; it does the spirit good. Ask Him to search your heart.

Cast—to cause to move or to send forth by throwing. God desires that we give Him all our cares. He said to *cast* all our cares on Him because He cares for us. Go ahead, *cast* it. God's an awesome catcher.

Presently, I am involved with two friends dealing with a complex situation, and their hearts are attached. As I listened intently to each of them, I knew immediately the hardest part would be "doing it." So I prayed that God would grant them both the spirit of LG. You know . . . LG. We all need it when we're in this kind of situation. I pray that a spirit of "Let Go" come upon you when you need it most.

As I pondered today's inspirational message, I asked Him what He wanted to say to you this morning. He said to me in the most loving, sweetest, and softest tone, "Tell them they are mine." One compliment deserves another, right? Sure. Now, tell Him, "I'm yours today."

While sitting in my room one morning, I heard people engaged in conversation; however, I did not recognize their voices. All of a sudden, I heard this loud sneeze and said, "That's my baby." He's six feet three inches, twenty-three years old. Sure enough it was, as he placed the key in the door to prove it was he. I wonder, if we recognize our Father's voice so readily and assuredly, how many problems could we have avoided? We can recognize His voice when He speaks to us by spending more time with Him like we do with our other interests.

While talking with my daughter this morning about her decision to being no longer the bigger person in reconciling some past mistreatment placed upon her by a family member, I replied in my sweet and loving, motherly tone, "Baby, you are never *wrong* for doing *right*." Keep the faith.

Allow God to open your eyes so you can see that there are more (angels) with you than enemies around you. I say you have the *victory*! Be glad about it!

Today, decide to believe in what you don't see or feel. Faith calls things that aren't as if they already exist. The next time you walk into that bad situation, call it good. Call your needs met. Call your dead dreams alive. You have what you say. I say I have everything I need, and my cup runs over. Goodness and mercy follow me all the days of my life. Care to join me in faith talk today?

My daughter and I were conversing about her future when I said to her, "Never ask your past what's in your future. Niki, *Don't* ask yesterday about tomorrow." It doesn't have the correct answer. Whenever you have a consultation with these "guys," you cheat yourself because today you are much different than you were yesterday. God says we move from glory to glory. We move from faith to faith. Better yet, God's mercies are new for us every morning. Remind yourself each day that you are not the same person you were yesterday. Today you are more insightful. Today you are different. Today you are more resourceful. Today you believe what God says about you.

God says in all things, give thanks, correct? If I walk outside and get hit by a truck, do I thank God for the hit or for surviving?

Since God has made His wonderful works to be remembered, is it okay for me to agree with God that *you* are *unforgettable*?

Preparing for battle is your part, but deliverance comes from the Lord. Do you trust Him? You can because He's mighty in battle.

I pray you never stop believing that a person can *change* for the better. I pray the *changes* you desperately need to improve your life happen as quickly as you believe. I pray your thoughts become like God's as you watch what *changes* all around you

Only look back to see how far He's brought you. Then let Him know how grateful you are that He didn't leave you the way He found you.

Have you ever been alone with God and said to Him, "I've been loved before, and I know what 'good' and 'sweet' love feels like; but no one has *ever* loved me like You." You've always been there for me. You held me together when I thought I was going to go crazy. In your presence is the only time I don't feel alone. What You give me, I've *never* received from anyone else before. So let me say, "Thank you." Such an inadequate word for such an awesome, amazing, wonderful, loving, and incredible God.

The Lord is on our side; we have nothing to fear. God will sustain us. Great and mighty is our God.

Whenever you feel like a loser, a failure, or that this time you won't recover, don't believe it. According to your faith, so be it unto you.

Today would be a good day to let that someone who's always there for you regardless of the time or circumstance know how you appreciate him or her. That person deserves to know how valuable he or she is to you.

Sometimes in life, we don't always have the answers to our setbacks. Nonetheless, we should keep moving; and perhaps while we are in motion, the answer with an understanding will come.

I can recall a time in my life when I struggled just to make it through the day. One particular morning when my adult children were still of elementary school age, I said to God with tears streaming down my face, "Father, this situation is so hard." He said to me, "The *harder* the trial, the *sweeter* the grace." I knew from that moment on I could make it, and I did.

Some days take *big* steps. On other days, take *baby* steps. However, there is *never* a day that you don't step. Keep going. It is worth it! (I did this one for you, and you know who you are.)

While in the ladies' room at work, I was standing in front of the mirror, preparing to ask God to make a situation work out for me just this one time, He answered me before I could complete my request. Mind you, this situation was bothersome and burdensome, but I was holding on to hope that it would be good for me. God said, "You can save yourself the pain. I'm only in what I ordain." Strong huh? Although I was disappointed, I obeyed. Today, I am so *happy*!

You can't give up now; look at how far you've come. No one knows better than you how hard you've tried. Your life is "to be continued".

I've learned to see God in everything. He's in that disappointing circumstance because He kept you from the worst of it. Acknowledge Him in the midst of your lowest times, and He'll lift you high enough so you can see what greatness awaits you on the other side.

At a very difficult time in my life, I asked my then five- and six-year-old children to help me. Their assignment was to tell me, "Mommy, you can make it." My daughter took that assignment to heart and would run inside the house from playing just to say, "Mommy, you can make it." I needed to hear those words just to get out of bed. I needed to hear those words at times just to stay alive. I encourage you to let your words be seasoned with grace. Your words are a lifeline. Someone is saying, "*Help*!"

I don't care what it looks like. I don't care how it feels. I don't care what they say. All I know is that I *believe* God! I believe God!

Do what you can do to help those in your life. Never let those you help make you feel responsible for their failure. It's a choice they make to fly or walk. God gave us all the ability to succeed.

My daughter was six years old and loved to climb into my bed. Exhausted from the day, I asked her if she wanted to go outside to play with her friend or in her room. She replied, "No, Mommy, I want to be with you." Determined to get my "me" time, I asked her to go to her room. Later, I noticed her standing at the door looking at me. I said, "Come to Mommy, baby." She jumped into bed and rewarded me with a smile, kiss, and hug. Then God said to me, "She desired nothing from you, only your presence. I too desire that you just want to *be* in My *presence.*"

My son and I were engaged in conversation about his plans for the future. He proceeded to tell me how discouraging it was for him when talking to certain people about his dreams for his life. I agreed and said, "Son, learn to recognize '*dream killers*' early, and remove yourself from them immediately." When God gives you a dream, you have a right to fight for it. Don't let anyone take that right away. Fight the *good fight* of faith then watch it happen. Now, let the church say *amen*!

When I went through the fire, He kept me cool. When the water was almost over my head, He didn't let me drown. When my heart was broken, He fixed it. When the load was too heavy, He carried it for me. *Thanks a million*. We all know who you are.

On my way home from work the other day, I wrote these words to God, "Lord, I remember how hard it used to be for me. Today, it's a lot easier, and I know it's because I'm learning I can rely on you. Sir, I could just smack myself for not knowing sooner how *credible* you are. Thanks for being aware of schemes and plots that are secretly being devised to discredit and destroy me. You always come through with the truth and deliverance. You are trustworthy. You are kind. You are perfect in all your ways. Because of Your greatness and bountiful love for me, I say thank you. Thanks for sticking with me when there was less adhesive holding us together from my side. Thanks for not letting me go."

I was walking through the mall one Saturday afternoon, thinking about my failures. From behind a partition, I could hear people talking while they worked on opening a new store. All of a sudden, God said, "Although you can't see what's going on behind that partition, likewise, I am at work in your life behind the scenes." The good work He started in you, He's able to finish.

"Mommy, are you crying?" My five-and-a-half-year-old daughter at the time asked me.

Discreetly wiping my eyes and face, I replied, "Mommy is okay." She then requested I give her a hug. After the tight, feel-so-good hug, she said, "Ump, I got it now, Mommy."

"Got what, baby?"

"Your pain. Do you feel better, Mommy?"

"Oh baby, Mommy feels so much better."

God can use the smallest one to bring the biggest help to you when you need it most.

Whenever my son leaves for work, he always says, "See ya. Ma, I love ya."

"I love you too, baby."

Hearing those words melt my heart every time. Only love knows its way around one's heart. Love will stay where it's respected. Never take the ones who love *you* for granted.

The decision you make to improve your life might not be popular or accepted among those you keep company. Sometimes, deciding to live the abundant life means *breaking* away so you can *fly* away. It's your life. He promised you "good success." You decide if you should soar or walk. Personally, I love the bird's-eye view.

He extended His hand out for me and helped me up. I said to Him, "I didn't see that coming, Lord. It felt like someone just came up from behind me, running full speed and knocked my feet from underneath me." The above scene came about at a time I thought I was *focused*. I was meeting *goals* and checking them off as I went along. I was making progress. Then all of a sudden, I allowed outside interference to take me off course. *How subtle*, I thought. It took me months to get back on track. You should always ask God's permission before you let someone dressed in "sheep's" clothing access the door of your life. You can forfeit and sometimes delay your destiny if you don't get with Him first. He's the *discerner* of one's heart and motives.

Today *is* the opportune time for you to make an intelligent decision to "step up," "step out," and "step on." You know what's required of you by Him. Your assignment is *not* about you. It's about a "people" you haven't met yet. It's about families who don't know if they are going to be together. It's about those waiting and praying for the light to shine in their dark place. Hurry! Get dressed and go to them! They've been anticipating your arrival.

God purposed that you fulfill your destiny. Along the way, you've grown weary, tired, uncertain and have lost the will. I am saying to *you* today, "*Press*! *Press* on, my brother! *Press* on, my sister! Fight the good fight of faith. The race isn't *won* by the fastest or the strongest *but* by the one who finishes the race. When you must, *rest* in the Lord, but you can't quit as there are too many lives attached to you and your destiny. Fight! Holler! Run! Swim! Walk! Jump! Crawl if you must, but get to your destiny. We need you!"

Have you ever just asked God to change you? There was a time in my life when I was just fed up with me. As I prayed, I saw God's feet and ankles. They were huge. As He was preparing to leave, I grabbed Him around His feet and said, "Please, God, change me! Please don't leave me this way, or I'll self-destruct!" I had grown tired of my selfish thoughts, ambitions, and desires. I had become cold, callous, and uncaring. It is me, oh Lord, standing in need of prayer. All He needs is an invitation, and He'll change you for the better.

As I pondered over a situation that left me broken, up from my spirit came these words, "I don't know *why* but I do know *how*. I know *how* to *proceed* (to continue after a *pause* or *interruption*). Thank you, Father God, for always reminding me that when I am cast down, I can *never ever* be destroyed. I will always advance with Your assistance. I am always triumphant through Him who loves me."

While sitting in solitude and despair, God asked me a question, "What are
you doing with your *life*?"

I replied, "I don't know, Lord."

He asked me:

      Are you, (L)iving
                (I)n
                (F)ear
                (E)very day,
    or are you
                (L)iving
                (I)n
                (F)aith
                (E)very day?

Choose LIFE, and He'll live in that world with you.

I pray all you have ever dreamed about that's grand and pure come to pass for you today. I pray as soon as you tell the devil to flee, he leaves. I pray you get a call from the banker saying, "Someone just deposited a million bucks into your account." I pray you bounce back quickly after fainting so you can *enjoy* it. I pray you allow the God of the Bible to *love* you in a way He's always wanted to. May this day be filled with peace, contentment, and hope for you and your family. I pray your enemy calls or stops by to apologize to you. I pray you release them from the guilt. I pray you are inspired to believe in all the possibilities in God. *Now*, is there *anything* too hard for the Lord?

After exiting my car, I noticed a man and a woman underneath some bushes taking a nap. They both were nestled close to each other while their skin lay almost bare on the pavement. This scene disturbed me for the rest of the day. I had questions like, who are their family and friends? Who do they love? Who loves them? I wondered if anyone dared to care. I wondered if anyone saw the breakdown happening but didn't have the courage to ask if they needed help. I know, some things we bring upon ourselves. Regardless, I still believe some things God allows so His love for humanity can be seen in how we respond to the down and out. My purpose for writing this inspirational is, so we will never forget the less fortunate. I hope we dare to care even when our pockets are empty. Have you ever entertained an angel unaware?

My mom would always say to our friends and us, "There's *good* in everybody." Although at times we would venture to convince her that the person we were talking about missed out on the good. After numerous discussions with my mom, I'd left her presence feeling like something was terribly wrong with her thinking. (Sorry, Ma.) Today, I understand her teachings. She was saying that when a person does bad things with his or her life and God responds to their situation, He first sees the good in that person. Then God works *all* things (bad, good, or indifferent) in the mix for our good and for His purpose. Thanks, Momma. I tried to teach your grandchildren the same.

May God be gracious to you today and give you what's good and perfect. I pray your blessings run over you. I hope your heartstrings sing the melody of the Lord throughout the day. May you feel good about yourself today. I pray you have someone in your life that you can tell the truth to and not be judged. I pray you see God in the land of the living. When it's all said and done, I pray your crown is the biggest, and you hear God say, "Well done, good and faithful servant. Enter into the joy of the Lord."

When the pressure becomes unbearable, don't give in to it. Never agree with defeat that you are defeated. *Defeat* . . . defeat!

The *best* day is the one you can still see on your *worst* day. The *sweetest* victory is when you taste the *bitterness* of defeat, yet you still believe that you are triumphant. God always sees you as a *winner* through Him and by Him. Will you agree with God?

Most Saturdays, Daddy would make us clean the church, and he would tell us God was going to pay us for our work. Somehow I knew that what we were doing had a greater meaning than just sacrificing a Saturday morning; however, I never imagined it would put an intense desire inside each of us to love God and to carefully attend to His people. Daddy was teaching us servanthood. He was teaching us how to serve mankind with love and respect. Daddy was teaching us how to give back unselfishly. Because of Daddy, I trust I serve each of you Monday through Friday with a clearer image of God's *great* love for you. I sure hope it comes across. Thanks, Daddy. I love you.

As she held me like I was her baby, I said, "It hurts. It hurts, I'm going to die. The pain, oh my God, this pain." She held me tighter and just let me cry. She said, "Ellie, I lost my husband too a few years ago."

"What can He do for this pain?" I asked.

"Huh? Can He do something with this pain? Tonight is our anniversary."

When I stopped asking *why* and *worshipped* Him, God broke His silence.

He said, "One day *soon*, you will know love, joy, and laughter again. I promise."

Worship is the password.

Perhaps today you feel like you've gone as far as the road will take you. Maybe it seems as soon as you are over one hurdle, there's another. Now you are so overwhelmed and wondering what's next. I have a suggestion and it helps me each time. Say to God, "Lead me to the rock that's higher than me." Once you are there in your spirit and mind, take a *long, hard* look at your promised land. Isn't it grand? Isn't it beautiful? Can you see yourself over there living the way God intended? Gosh, look at you. Can you believe it? As far as your eyes can see belongs to you. Who you are is what you think in your heart. I say there *are* better days just around the horizon for you.

May you discover, after all the dust settles, that God never left you. I pray your children rise and call you blessed. I pray each adult child write you a check. I hope you feel the strength of God in a way you never have felt before. I pray, when there is nothing else you can say or do about your situation, that you will turn it over to God and trust Him to make it right. I pray you learn to dance in advance before you see the victory. I pray you laugh at the devil when you realize how he tried to handle a *child of God*. God desires to show Himself strong on our behalf. Will you let Him?

May you feel God's huge arms tightly around you today as He gently says, "I stayed awake all night watching over the things that you will deal with today. I waited for you to awake so you could experience another day of My peace and victory." Anything less is a counterfeit. He's the real One.